How to Draw
Ferocious
Dinosaurs
and Other Prehistoric Creatures

BARRON'S

Created and produced by Green Android Ltd

Illustrated by Fiona Gowen

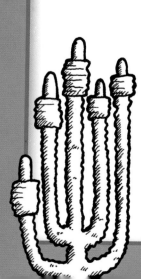

First edition for North America
published in 2016 by
Barron's Educational Series, Inc.

Copyright © Green Android Ltd 2016

Green Android Ltd
49 Beaumont Court
Upper Clapton Road
London. E5 8BG
www.greenandroid.co.uk

All inquiries should be addressed to:
Barron's Educational Series, Inc.
250 Wireless Boulevard
Hauppauge, NY 11788
www.barronseduc.com

ISBN: 978-1-4380-0852-3

Date of Manufacture:
January 2016
Manufactured by:
Toppan Leefung Printing Co., Ltd.,
Shenzhen, China

Printed in China
9 8 7 6 5 4 3 2 1

Contents

 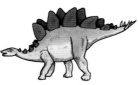
Page 32 has an index of everything to draw in this book.

Apex Predators

Many species of Therapod dinosaurs are apex predators, meaning they are at the top of their food chain. The 43 ft (13 m) Allosaurus was a fierce and aggressive hunter.

1 Draw the Allosaurus's tail, back, and part of the underbody.

2 Add the leg that is placed on the ground, then add the raised leg. Draw the chest and neck.

3 Draw the head with its strong jaws and large teeth, then draw a nostril and a small eye.

4 Midway down the chest, draw the arms ending in three fingers with sharp claws.

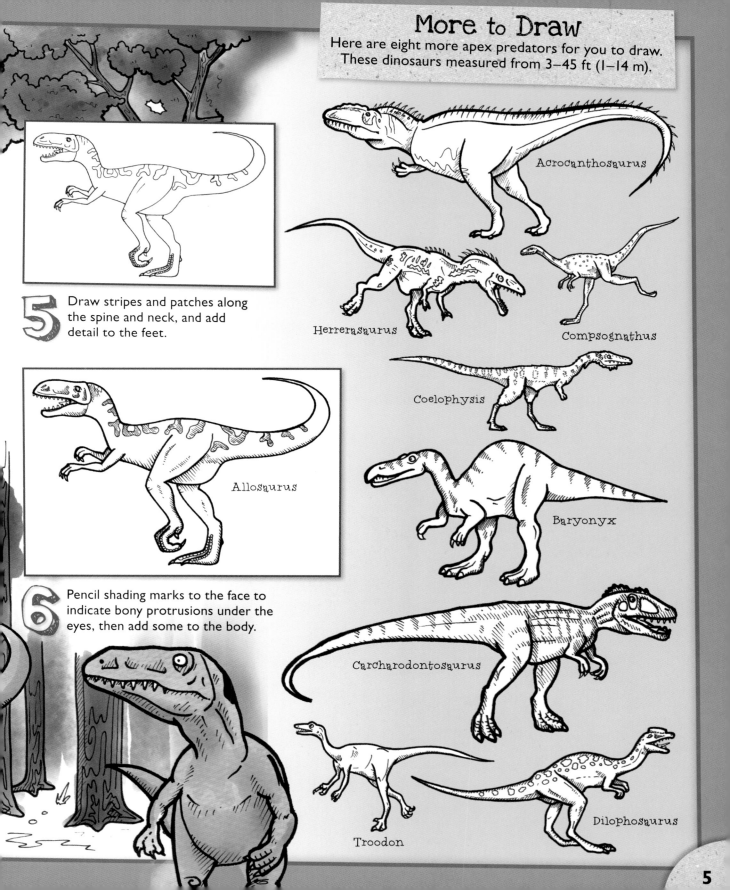

Here are eight more apex predators for you to draw.
These dinosaurs measured from 3–45 ft (1–14 m).

Acrocanthosaurus

Herrerasaurus

Compsognathus

5 Draw stripes and patches along the spine and neck, and add detail to the feet.

Coelophysis

Allosaurus

Baryonyx

6 Pencil shading marks to the face to indicate bony protrusions under the eyes, then add some to the body.

Carcharodontosaurus

Troodon

Dilophosaurus

5

How to Draw

Plant-eaters

The plant-eating (herbivore) dinosaurs were the largest animals to ever walk on Earth. The Diplodocus, like fellow herbivores, has a small head, long neck, and bulky body.

1 Draw the Diplodocus's long flexible tail and back.

2 Add the back legs and more of the underbody.

3 Pencil the front legs and the chest.

4 Draw the long neck — it is almost twice as long as the body — and the small head.

5 Sketch bulk at the top of the back leg, and draw other body and head details.

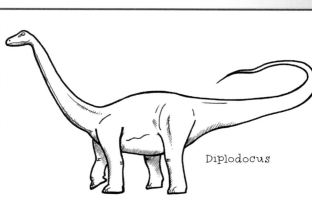

Diplodocus

6 Add shading to the neck, chest, legs, and tail.

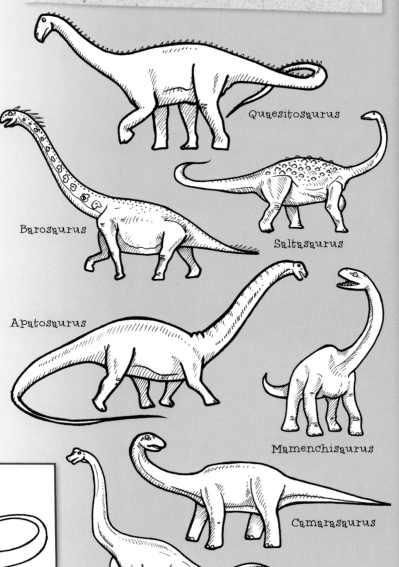

Quaesitosaurus

Barosaurus

Saltasaurus

Apatosaurus

Mamenchisaurus

Camarasaurus

Brachiosaurus

Paralititan

Amargasaurus

7

How to Draw
Terrifying T. rex

The Tyrannosaurus rex — the tyrant lizard — was strong, quick, and ferocious. It could tear off and chew over 500 lbs (230 kg) of meat with one bite of its jaws. It was 40 ft (12 m) long.

1 Draw the top of the T. rex's upper jaw and head, its back, and its tail.

2 Add the rest of its strong jaws and gaping mouth.

3 Add two puny arms, each with two clawed fingers.

4 Draw an eye, the back leg that is placed on the ground — ending in three clawed toes — and then the other leg.

Tyrannosaurus rex

5 Sketch lots of bone-crushing teeth, and add details to the eye and nostril.

6 Complete the Tyrannosaurus rex by pencilling some shading to the front of the body and to the powerful legs.

Horn-faced Dinos

The Ceratopsian dinosaurs, with their frilled necks and horns, were herding herbivores. When the herd was threatened these car-sized dinosaurs would charge the predator.

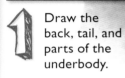

1 Draw the back, tail, and parts of the underbody.

2 Add the short, strong legs starting with the back legs first.

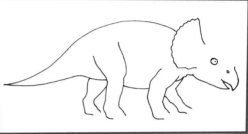

3 Sketch in the frill, then the lower jaw and beaked mouth. Draw a nostril and an eye.

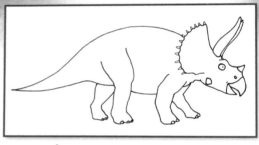

4 Draw two curved horns and the stubby horn. Fill in the rest of the head and details.

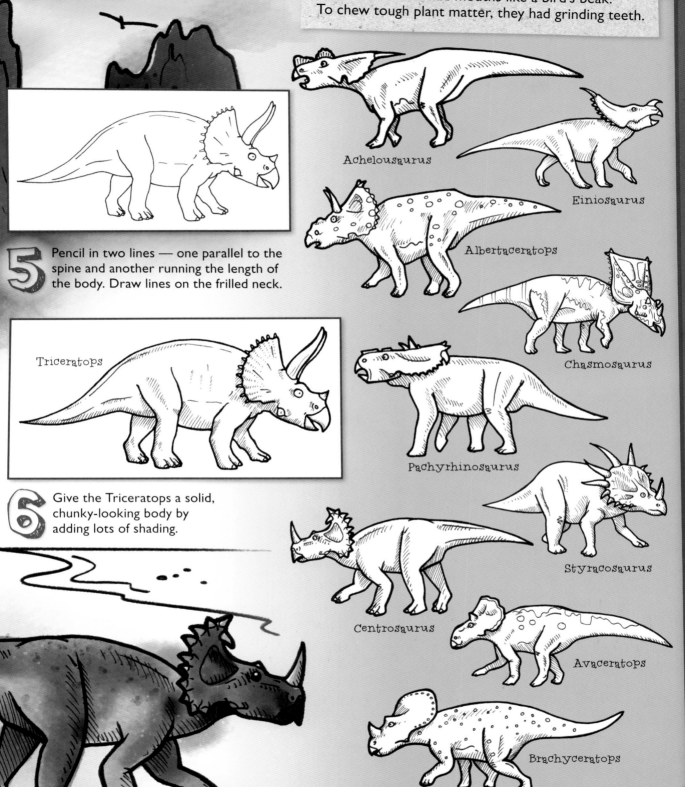

More to Draw
Plant-eaters had mouths like a bird's beak.
To chew tough plant matter, they had grinding teeth.

5 Pencil in two lines — one parallel to the spine and another running the length of the body. Draw lines on the frilled neck.

Triceratops

6 Give the Triceratops a solid, chunky-looking body by adding lots of shading.

Achelousaurus

Einiosaurus

Albertaceratops

Chasmosaurus

Pachyrhinosaurus

Styracosaurus

Centrosaurus

Avaceratops

Brachyceratops

Armor-plated

The 30-ft (9-m) long Stegosaurus was a herbivore that took self-defense to a new level. It had 17 bony plates along its back, and its strong tail was spiked.

1 Draw the underbody, tail, and back.

2 Add the legs — the back legs are twice as tall as the front legs. Then, add the feet and the tiny head.

3 Draw two pairs of spikes on the tail.

4 Sketch in 10 triangular plates along the Stegosaurus's spine.

5 Draw seven more bony plates, and add detail to the head.

Stegosaurus

6 Add shading to the plates, legs, and underbody to give the Stegosaurus some bulk.

How to Draw
Giant Meat-eater

The Giganotosaurus was a shark-toothed carnivore that could chase down prey at speeds of 30 miles (50 km) per hour. Its huge head was larger than a human!

1 Draw the thin tail, back, neck, and part of the underbody.

2 Sketch the Giganotosaurus's huge head and open mouth.

3 Draw a tiny arm ending with three clawed fingers.

4 Draw an eye, nostril, and long legs with clawed toes.

5 Add triangular-shaped stripes to the head and upper body.

Giganotosaurus

6 Sketch in shading on the underbody and legs to give the Giganotosaurus shape.

How to Draw
Raging Raptors

The feather-covered raptors are among the best-known of all dinosaurs. The Velociraptor, known as the speedy thief, could run up to 40 miles (60 km) per hour to catch plant-eating prey.

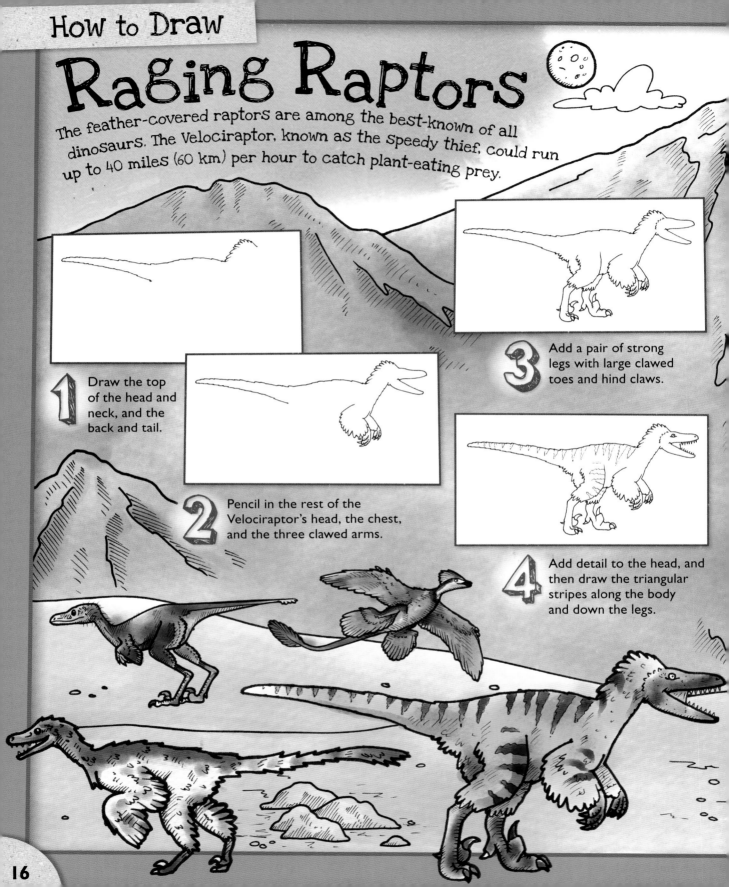

1 Draw the top of the head and neck, and the back and tail.

2 Pencil in the rest of the Velociraptor's head, the chest, and the three clawed arms.

3 Add a pair of strong legs with large clawed toes and hind claws.

4 Add detail to the head, and then draw the triangular stripes along the body and down the legs.

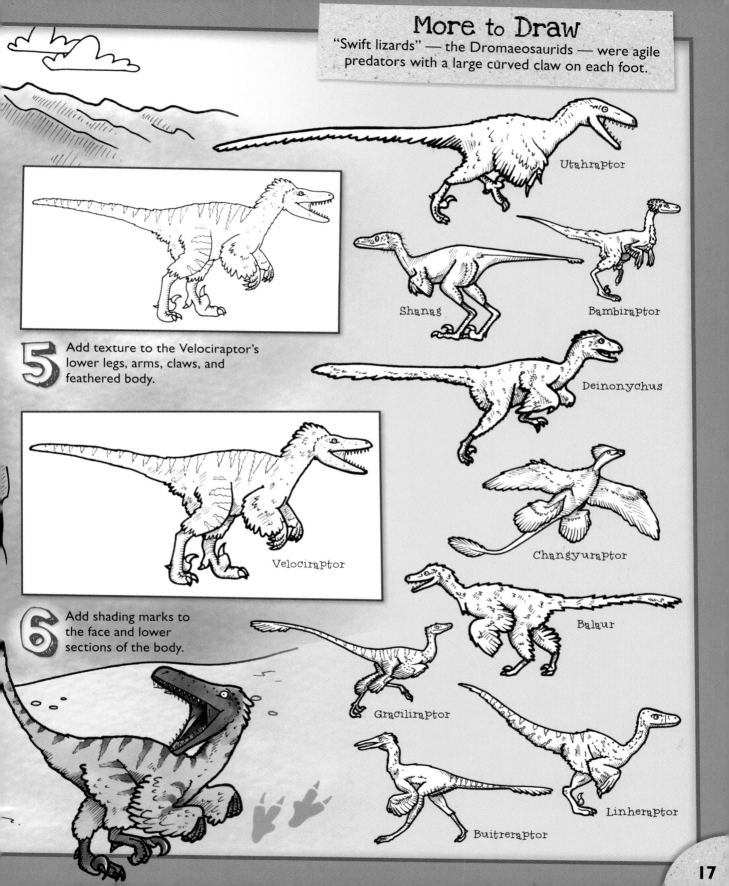

Utahraptor

Shanag

Bambiraptor

5 Add texture to the Velociraptor's lower legs, arms, claws, and feathered body.

Deinonychus

Velociraptor

Changyuraptor

6 Add shading marks to the face and lower sections of the body.

Balaur

Graciliraptor

Linheraptor

Buitreraptor

How to Draw
Handy Iguanodon

This 40-ft (12-m) long herbivore dinosaur had hands that each had four fingers — the little fingers were very long — and a spiked thumb. It could walk on two or four limbs.

1 Draw the back and tail.

2 Add the Iguanodon's neck and small head.

3 Draw long back legs, each ending with three clawed toes.

4 Pencil in the arms. Add four fingers and spiked thumbs to each one.

Iguanodon

5 Add details to the head, and draw lines to indicate bulkiness.

6 Shade the Iguanodon's underbody, flank, legs, arms, neck, and head.

How to Draw

Flying Reptiles

Pterosaurs ruled the skies in the Mesozoic period. The smaller species flapped their wings, while the largest ones soared using wind currents. They are not related to birds and bats.

1 Draw the Hatzegopteryx's long beak, head, and underbody.

2 Add one long wing with three wing fingers. This large reptile had a 16 ft (5 m) wingspan.

3 Draw a leg ending with three clawed toes.

More to Draw
Winged lizards were sparrow- to airplane-sized.
They had large brains, good eyesight, and ate meat.

4 Sketch in the Hatzegopteryx's second leg and wing.

5 Add detail to the beak and head, and pencil in the arm that forms the wing.

6 Shade in the underbody and wings to give this flying meat-eater texture and shape.

Pterodaustro

Cearadactylus

Sordes

Rhamphorhynchus

Dsungaripterus

Dimorphodon

Scaphognathus

Hatzegopteryx

Quetzalcoatlus

Anurognathus

21

How to Draw

Sea Monsters

These marine beasts include species that resemble modern day bony fish, molluscs, turtles, and even dolphins. But one thing is certain — they were all fearsome oceanic predators!

1 Draw the tail fin and upper body of the Thalattoarchon.

2 Add the head and dolphin-like snout.

3 Pencil in a flipper and second smaller fin.

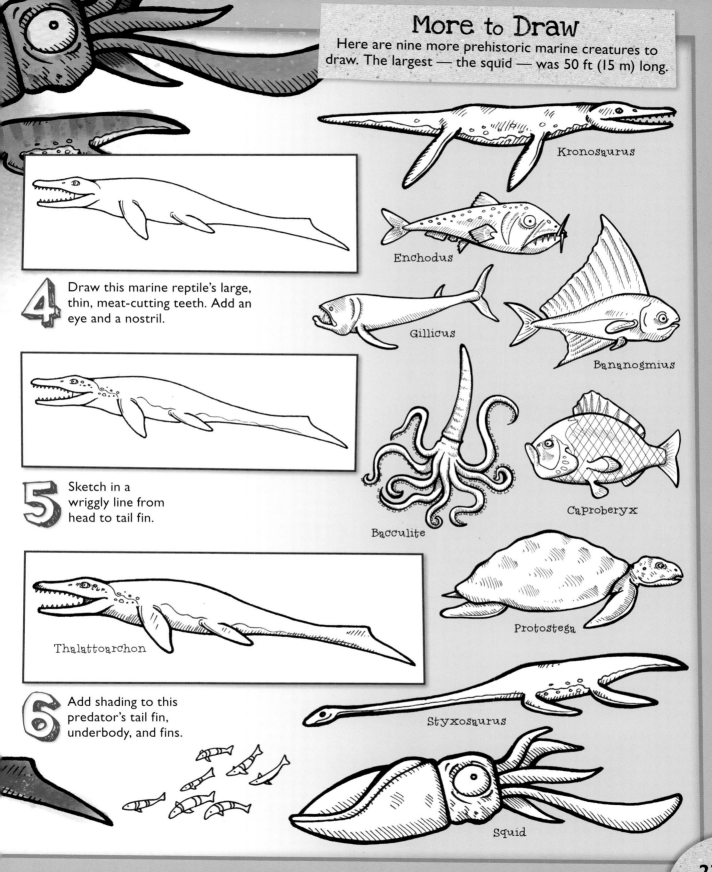

More to Draw

Here are nine more prehistoric marine creatures to draw. The largest — the squid — was 50 ft (15 m) long.

Kronosaurus

Enchodus

Gillicus

Bananogmius

Bacculite

Caproberyx

Protostega

Styxosaurus

Squid

Thalattoarchon

4 Draw this marine reptile's large, thin, meat-cutting teeth. Add an eye and a nostril.

5 Sketch in a wriggly line from head to tail fin.

6 Add shading to this predator's tail fin, underbody, and fins.

Amazing Mammoth

The last woolly mammoth died out only 4,000 years ago, and frozen carcasses have been found in Siberia, Russia. Covered in fur, it stood 11 ft (3.4 m) tall.

1 Draw the rear and back of the mammoth.

2 Using a wriggly line, draw a back leg, shaggy underbody, and front leg.

3 Draw the chest, head, and trunk. Then, draw a small ear and an eye.

4 Now, draw enormous curved and pointed tusks. The tusks could grow to 16 ft (5 m)!

5 Sketch short lines to give the impression of the mammoth's long, hairy coat.

Woolly mammoth

6 Add lots of shading to the underbody, legs, and tusk of this extraordinary animal.

Saber-toothed Cats

These cats had prominent canine teeth — some which grew all through the animal's life — that were used to inflict a fatal wound to prey, which included our early ancestors!

1 Draw the Smilodon's back and snout.

2 Draw the short but strong back legs and the underbody.

3 Now, add the front legs — note the large paws — and chest.

4 Draw the tail, an ear, the backward curving fang, and other facial features.

5 Sketch spots on the upper body and add some tiger-like stripes to the front leg and the head.

Smilodon

6 Pencil shading to the inside of the Smilodon's legs, its underbody, and chest.

Dinofelis

Wakaleo

Dinictis

Thylacosmilus

Barbourofelis

Proailurus

Nimravus

Pseudaelurus

Eusmilus

27

How to Draw

Roaming Reptiles

Land-dwelling reptiles — prehistoric crocodiles, snakes, turtles and lizards — lived before and alongside the dinosaurs. Megalania was a 18 ft (5.5 m) giant goanna with venom glands.

1 Draw the Megalania's long upper body and tail.

2 Add the head, long jaws, and neck.

3 Draw the stubby front legs and the rest of the underbody.

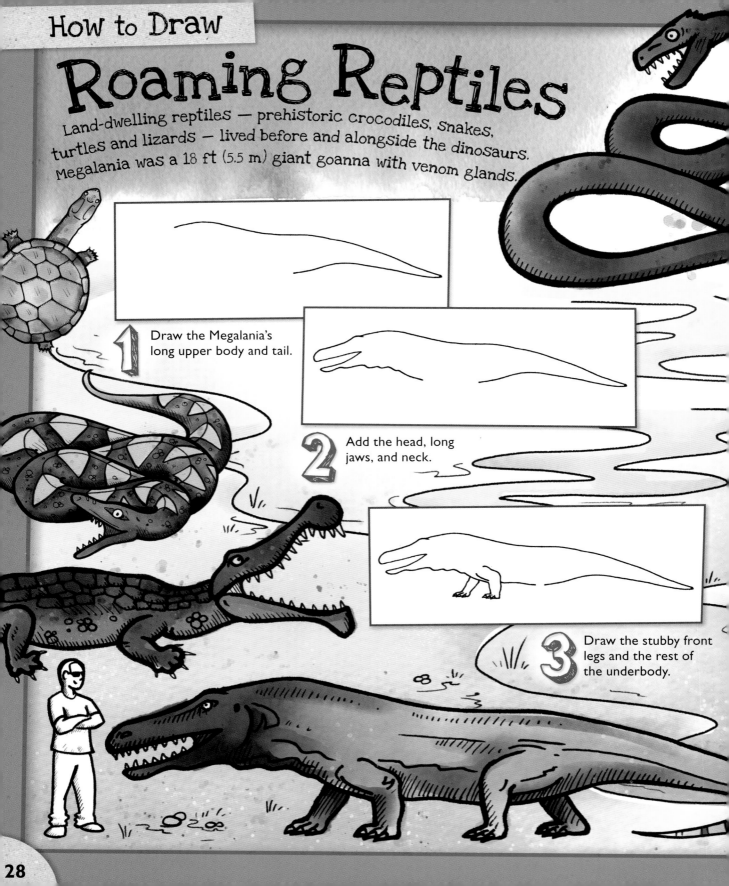

28

The smallest of these prehistoric reptiles was only 12 in (30 cm); the largest — a snake — was 43 ft (13 m)!

Chimaerasuchus

Haasiophis

Archelon

Titanoboa

4 Now, pencil in the back legs. All the legs end in clawed toes.

Eunotosaurus

Puentemys

5 Draw the teeth, a nostril, and an eye. Draw rough lines to give the Megalania some shape.

Madtsoia

Megalania

6 Sketch shading on the snout, underbody, and on the legs.

Sarcosuchus

Arizonasaurus

29

How to Draw
Unique Ratfish

The Helicoprion is a prehistoric ratfish with a unique set of teeth. Up to 150 teeth in a circular saw arrangement on the lower jaw caught and cut up soft-bodied prey like squid.

1 Draw a shark-like torpedo-shaped body and tail fin.

2 Complete the underbody and draw the jaws and mouth.

3 Draw the teeth wheel, eye, nostril, and gill cover. Finish the tail fin.

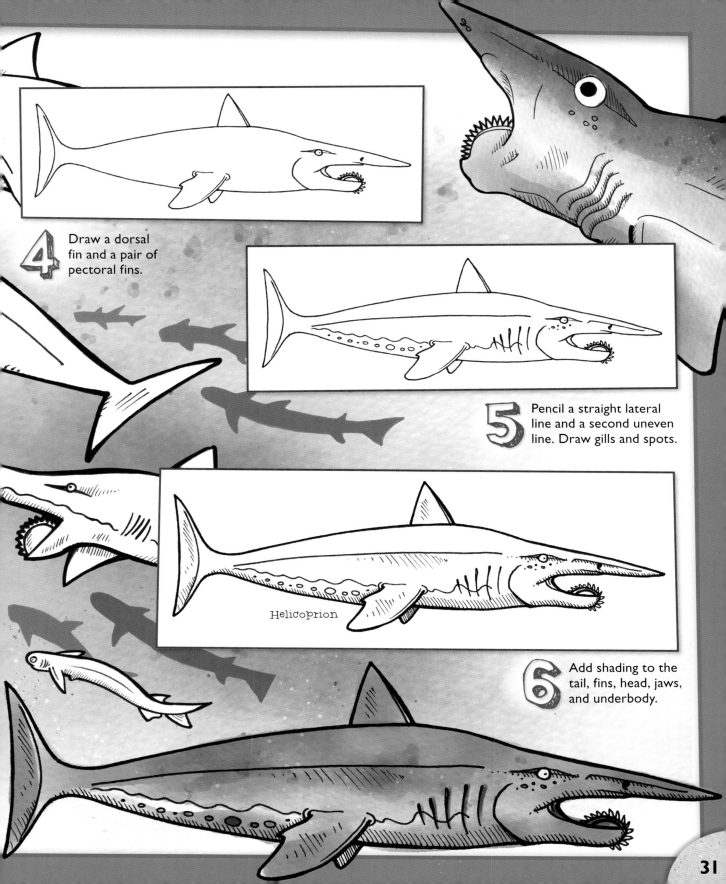

4 Draw a dorsal fin and a pair of pectoral fins.

5 Pencil a straight lateral line and a second uneven line. Draw gills and spots.

Helicoprion

6 Add shading to the tail, fins, head, jaws, and underbody.

Index

This index lists in alphabetical order all the prehistoric beasts that appear in this book so it will be easy to find all your favorites!

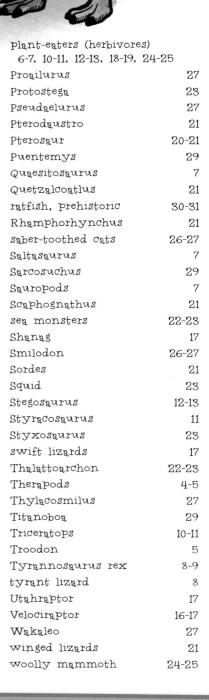

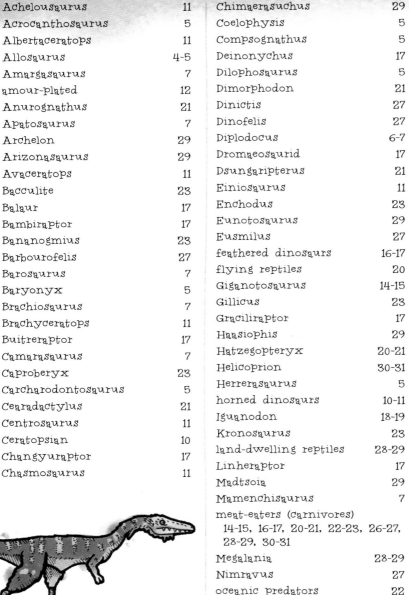